P9-ECL-661

MINECRAFT

A Beginner's Guide
2nd Edition

David Oconner

©Copyright 2013 David Oconner

ISBN-13: 978-1481833035

Table of Contents

Minecraft

History

Minecraft is block-infested sandbox building/exploring game developed by Mark Persson, aka 'Notch', and his company, Mojang AB. The 'full version' or Minecraft has been available on PC since November 18th, 2011, but the game has been popular since Beta testing opened to players in 2009.

Controls

Esc - Pause/Menu

Left Mouse Button – Primary Action (Dig/Chop/Attack) ; Single-tap – Toggle Doors/Switches

Right Mouse Button – Secondary Action (Use/Place Block/Interact/Eat)

WASD – Move/Strafe (Double-tap 'W' to Sprint)

Space – Jump (Can be held)

Mouse – Look

Left Shift – Sneak (Also keeps you from accidentally falling)

'E' – Inventory

Mouse Button 3 ('Mouse Scroll Button') – Cycle through inventory (1-9)

'Q' – Drop Item

Tab – (Multiplayer) – Players List

HUD

Heads Up Display

1) Health – Shown by hearts – Hearts are removed when damage is taken from: falling, monster attacks, fire/lava, poison, explosions and drowning/suffocating.

2) Armour – Shown as little grey tunics above your health – Armour icons only show up when you're wearing protective, craftable armour, made of leather, iron, gold, or diamond. Each armour icon indicates how much damage will be absorbed from attacks (damage from drowning, fire, suffocation are not reduced). Each tunic indicates about an 8% decrease in damage taken.

3) Hunger – Shown by 'drumsticks' – Indicates how 'full' you are – When you are full (or nearly full) you will regenerate health as normal and can sprint – When your hunger gets low, you will no longer regenerate health (hearts) or be able to sprint. You become hungry at a slow rate as you play, but some actions make you hungrier faster, like: attacking, sprinting and jumping

4) Experience – The Green bar with sections – the number in the middle indicates what 'Level' you are. You gain experiences by killing monsters/animals, shown as little green orbs that drop when they die. You can use experience to enchant your tools and

items. (See the enchanting section for more details.)

5) Inventory Quick-slots: The 9 empty boxes in your inventory can be filled with any item in your inventory and is useful for quickly switching between regularly used items, like cobblestone, pickaxes or food. You can access each slot by pressing its corresponding number key (1-9) or by using the mouse wheel (mouse button 3) to cycle through the quick-slots.

6) Air -Only shown while underwater/suffocating- Bubbles will appear above your 'Hunger' icons. These show you how much air you have left. When you run out of air, you'll start taking drowning damage at the rate of roughly 1 heart-per-second. Get your head above water to get more air. You can also suffocate by being crushed by sand, your hearts reducing quickly.

Minecraft Basics

So what the heck can I do in this weird, block-ridden game?

Placing and Picking up Blocks

Most blocks in Minecraft can be picked up, but not always by hand. You'll need special tools to extract precious ores or till the earth to make your first farm. In general, though left-click will dislodge blocks and right-click will place them. (You can hold down either for automatic mining/digging/chopping or placement.)

Craft tools and weapons and collect and manufacture your own building materials

Make axes, picks, shovels, swords and more from stone, iron, diamond and even gold!

Explore the snow and ice, mountainous ranges, the seashore, swamp or forests!

Each area has unique plants and animals!

Above ground you'll find various biomes with plants and animals that only grow/appear in specific regions. Explore snow-covered peaks; blistering, cactus-filled deserts; dense jungles, lush forests and more!

Delve deep underground

Uncover abandoned mineshaft, rare ruined fortresses and deep ravines that expose precious blocks to fearless spelunkers.

There are treasures in the earth, if you know where to look. Strip abandoned mineshafts bare of old rails and be on the look out for aggressive cave spiders!

Explore other dimension.

But be careful, below the bedrock of the surface lies the fiery 'Nether', accessible only through specially-prepared portals. You'll find nether-only blocks and items, fearsome zombie-pigs, massive ghasts, magma cubes and fireball throwing blazes. Explore sprawling nether-fortresses, if you dare: the Nether is not for the faint-hearted.

Can you find 'The End'?

The mysterious Endermen hold the key to the terminal region of Minecraft's gameworld. Explore the Nether for the other piece of the key to activate long-abandoned portals, but beware: there is no turning back.

Your First Day

You're safe during the daylight hours in Minecraftia, but the night is full of danger! Let's get started!

Simple Dirt Marker

Take a moment to get your bearings. The place where you first enter the gameworld is called your 'spawn point'. This is where you'll respawn if you happen to perish (before you sleep in a bed, more on that later) due to an untimely fall or a zombie ambush. Take a look around and try and find some unique landmarks. Until you build some markers of your own, it's very easy to get lost.

Don't stray too far from your spawn, just yet. Until you have some tools and shelter ready, stay within viewing distance of where you first entered the game. When you die in Minecraft, you'll drop all your items and lose your accumulated experience before you respawn. Dropped items decay (disappear from the game forever) about 5 minutes after they leave your inventory, so it's important that you not stray too far. It's nerve-wracking to have only only precious seconds to locate and recover your tools and block before they are gone forever because you died too far from your spawn.

Keep an eye on the sky. Minecraftia's sun travels from east to west, just like our own, but it does so much faster than ours: a day is only 10 minutes long! When the sun is directly overhead, you'll know you only have about 5 minutes until sundown. Work quickly!

Okay! I know where I am and that time is short! What now?

Trees

One word: Wood. Your #1 priority should be to procure a good source of lumber from (hopefully) nearby trees . If you've spawned in a forest or mountainous area you should find some nearby (remember to turn up your view distance if you're having trouble). If not, you may have to scout the area to find some lumber.

Okay, you found a tree: now punch it! (Hint: click and hold your Left Mouse buttons for optimal tree-punching). After a few hits, you should have a block of wood! Congrats! Gather up a couple trees' worth of blocks (10 or so blocks) and we'll move on:

Inventory Use And Crafting

Press 'E' and open up for inventory. It should look something like this:

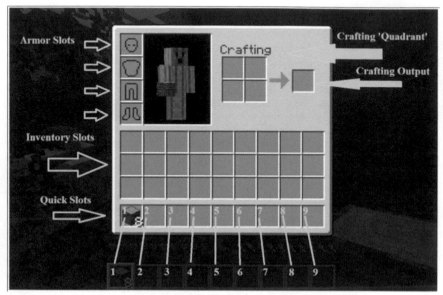

Heads Up Display

Once your inventory is open you'll see a couple different sections: in the mid-left, you'll see your character. To the left of that you'll see the 4 armor slots, arranged vertically. This is where you can put on craftable armor-pieces that can shield you from damage. Below your character will be 30 inventory slots. This is where you'll carry all your blocks, items, armor, food and everything else you can carry. Below the inventory slots are your quick-use slots. You'll want to put items you use frequently here so you can access them without having open up your inventory. (Put the items you use more in the 1, 2, 3, 4 slots, as they are going to be the easiest to reach, just above your left-hand on the WASD controls.)

To the right of your character is the crafting-quadrant. (Really, just 4 slots, but 'quadrant' sounds cooler) You can craft small items within your inventory by placing different items in the proper configurations in craft-quadrant and, if you've got the crafting recipe right, the new item to be crafted will appear on the single box to the right of the arrow.

The recipe we are interested in now is the '*Workbench*'. To make a workbench, you'll need 4 wooden planks. How do you get wooden planks? Put that wood we cut down earlier in the crafting-quadrant – it becomes 4 planks of wood!

Planks Of Wood

Well done! Now, put one plank of wood in each of the four quadrants – you can now make a workbench! Click on the bench to create it, then place it in your inventory.

Crafting Table

The workbench is where you'll make most of your tools, weapons, armor and more. There are dozens of recipes, and some even work with different components, for now, let's just focus on the one we need: a pickaxe.

To make a *pickaxe*, we'll need 3 planks of wood and two sticks. You already know how to make that, so go ahead and turn the rest of your gathered wood into planks. Now, we need sticks: stack 2 plank of wood vertically on top of one another, so they're occupying 2 slots – viola! Sticks! Make sure you make a least 3.

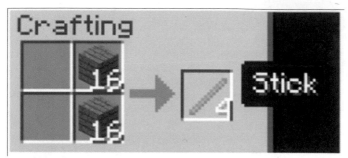

Sticks

Let's go ahead and place that Workbench. Don't worry too much about where, you can pick it up when you're done, if you want.

After it's placed, right click on it. You should see a a crafting-quadrant, except with 6 slots, (a crafting sextant?). This is where you'll make most of your tools, weapons, building materials, etc. For now, let's get that pickaxe made. Take your sticks and your wood planks and arrange them like so: Click on the pick! You can now mine!

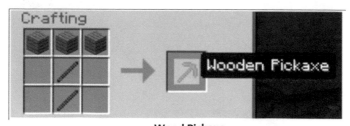

Wood Pickaxe

Let's get to digging! Start digging one block down, then forward, then down then forward. Digging like this makes a nice natural staircase to the surface, and it keeps you from falling to your door should you open up a natural cavern beneath your blocky feet. Keep digging until you reach Stone. It looks like this:

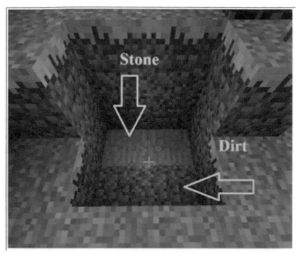

Stone vs Dirt

Mine about 2 dozen or so blocks and then head back to your craft bench (or drop it, if you've picked it up). It's time to upgrade your tools! Go ahead and make another pickaxe, but, this time, replace the Wood Planks with Cobblestone. There you go! You've made a Stone Pickaxe!

Stone Pickaxe

Stone tools dig/cut/chop/scoop faster than Wooden tools and also last longer! (Then next tool upgrade is Iron, but let's not worry about that, for now.)

Let's make a Stone Shovel, a Stone Axe (for cutting wood) and a Stone Sword, for fighting off monsters in the dark.

Stone Shovel

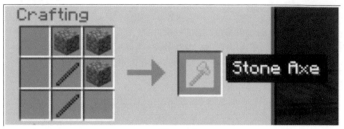

Stone Axe

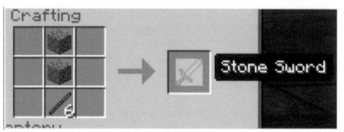

Stone Sword

Now that we've got some tools, let's start taming the darkness.

Let There Be Light

There are several types of light sources in Minecraft, but the one we're most concerned about now (and the one you're sure to use most of the time) is: Torches. Torches are made of sticks and coal, like so:

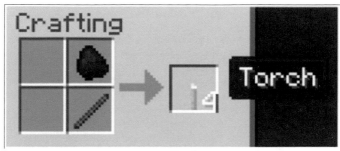

Torch

(The recipe for torches is small enough that you can make them easily without a workbench.)

You already know how to get sticks, so let's find coal. This is what you're looking for:

Coal

Coal is found anywhere you find Stone. If you're spawned in a hilly or mountainous area, you might luck out and be able to see coal seams on the surface. If not, scout around your immediate area and look for some easily accessible Coal blocks. If not, it's time to dig. Use the same Dig Down/Dig Forward/Dig Down routine as before. This will keep you safe from deadly falls and able to climb back up easily.

If you've got a reasonable supply of coal (20-30 pieces), you're ready to start building your first shelter! (If no coal is visible anywhere, head back and start chopping down some more trees. It's a little time-consuming, but we can make charcoal, instead. We'll see how in a minute.)

Your First Shelter

Now that you've got your tools and some torches, let's get you a base camp set up. What we want to accomplish with this first house is to keep you safe during the night, set up a compact workstation, complete with a Workbench, at least one Furnace/Smelter, and a couple storage Chests, and then we can start on your first mineshaft!

A great site for your first shelter will be:
- At least a few blocks away from water (Avoid those pesky floods!),
- A few blocks away from any obvious cliffs or caverns,
- Preferably away from sand (Digging can be slow and falling sand can suffocate you!),
- Visible from spawn and from multiple angles,
- Near at least one or two trees,
- Within walking distance of a water source.

Build your shelter out of either cobblestone or wood planks. Why? Neither of these blocks are found underfoot, are easily to see from a distance and are good at resisting explosive damage (oh, and there will be explosions!) if you get lost or are returning from a long expedition.

Build the outside walls as a 5x5 square perimeter, with one column open where you want your door to go. After you've finished the first level, hop on top of the wall and build another two blocks high, it should look like this (I used cobblestone):

Wall

Hop down into the structure and fill in the top level above you. Once you've added this ceiling, drop your Workbench and we'll craft a Furnace, like so:

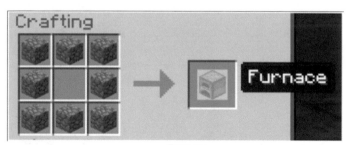

Furnace

Furnaces are used to cook food, smelt ore into useful metal, make glass and more. After the Workbench, Furnaces are probably the most import block in Minecraft. If you're lacking coal (or just curious), make some charcoal now with Wood Planks and Wood, here:

Charcoal

Let there be light! Go ahead and open up your inventory or Workbench and make some torches, if you haven't already. Put one or two inside your new house and one on each of the outer sides.

By now, the sun is probably setting and your doorway is bare! Let's get you a door! Craft one with 6 planks of Wood in this configuration:

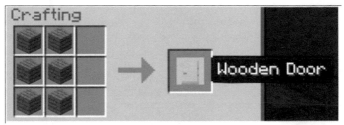

Wooden Door

Select the Door and right-click on the empty ground in your doorway. There we go! It's a bit cramped, but it's home.

Safe from the Darkness... Now what? Now that you're safe, let's talk about what goes bump in the dark.

Monsters

I told you nighttime was scary, right? Here's why: *monsters*. You may be able to explore and build without a care during the daytime (unless you fall off something high or set yourself on fire or... just be careful, okay?), but at night the is filled with things that want you dead.

Why the night? Monsters in Minecraft spawn (pop into the word) in low-light conditions. When you finally start mining, you'll find caves and even your mineshafts crawling with baddies, if you're not careful. Staying it well-lit areas, like your house (you did remember to put torches out, right?) will keep you safe, but you can't cower in your house forever. Let's see what you're up against:

Creepers: The deadliest thing on 4-legs; these green, eye-less monsters are silent until they're within arm's reach... and by then it's too late! Creepers are the suicide bombers of Minecraftia. They don't 'attack', per se, but sneak up on unwary miners and explore, destroying nearby blocks and objects. The only sounds creepers make is when they fall far enough to far damage, or when they emit their tell-tale 'hiiisssss', just before they explode. Either kill them from a distance with your bow or use hit-and-run knockback attacks (double tap 'forward' and attack while running) to wear down their health without staying close enough for them to explode! (Creepers can linger even after the sun comes up. Keep an eye out!)

Skeletons: : The dead walk... and shoot a bow? Skeletons come from out of the darkness with an urge to practice their undead archery on you, if you come too close! These skeletal archers can be dangerous for a couple reasons: all they need is line-of-site to pelt you with arrows that cause damage and knockback from over a dozen blocks away.

Single skeletons are a nuisance, but if you're caught out in the open, you can soon have arrows coming from all directions! Either rush into melee range and start hacking at them with your sword, or tactically return fire with your own bow to stop them.

Skeletons cannot survive in direct sunlight, but will retreat under trees and in water during the day. Like zombies, skeletons are happy to pick up any armour they find laying around, which gives them the same protection it affords you. Be wary of charging a skeleton in diamond armour with low health, unless you want to add it its collection.

Zombies: Like zombies everywhere else, these guys just want to walk straight for you and eat your brains. Zombies will take the most straight-forward path towards you and won't stop until you're dead! A few arrows or sword-hits will drop them, but they usually aren't alone. Dispatch them quickly to avoid becoming surrounded. (Like Skeletons, Zombies will die in direct sunlight. Thankfully, they aren't nearly as good at finding shade.)

Like skeletons, zombies can spawn with iron, gold or chainmail armor and weapons and make use of the added offence and defence these items give. If you die to a pack of zombies (or skeletons) hightail it back to where you died as fast as you can, but be prepared to contend against your monster murderers who have helped themselves to your fashionable armor in the meantime.

Spiders: These 8-legged menaces can't fit through small doorways, but they don't need to: they can just climb over the walls! Spiders can sense you behind walls and will climb up and over to pounce on you! Pelting these hissing arachnids with arrows from your bow is your best-bet. They are a wider than other monsters and not terribly fast and easy to hit. Spiders become non-aggressive in daylight.

Endermen: The rare Enderman (singular) is passive, but creepily tall creature. They will generally ignore you and busy themselves by moving single blocks around seemingly at random, as long as you don't look them in the eyes. Once you make eye-contact, be ready to fight! Endermen pack a serious punch and can teleport short distances and have no problem appearing behind you to attack. Make sure you're armored before you try to ambush one: they can't be killed by arrows (they just teleport out of the way) and hit hard, so make sure you're ready for an intense battle. Endermen are damaged by water and will quickly teleport to safety when it rains.

Witches: They (this picture notwithstanding) spend their entire cranky, pointy-hatted lives lurking in the swamps of Minecraftia. Despite their harmless-looking appearance, these single-warted foes (check the nose) are pretty tough to best in 1-on-1 combat. Once you get their attention, they show off both their alchemy skills and their throwing arm and will continually pelt you with potions of slow, poison, weakness and damage. Stay out of range of those potions and try and show her you're no slouch with a bow. A few arrows just below her fancy hat and you can swoop in and take all the rare alchemical goodies she drops. Take a second to search her wooden hut for more potion parts

Underground

You'll be stalked by skeletons, creepers and zombies underground, but there are a few monsters that only dwell deep beneath the earth.

Slimes

Slimes

Slimes are very rare, and fairly harmless, but they're persistent. Slimes only spawn very deep underground and come in a variety of sizes. Most slimes are smaller than you, but massive versions exist that can be the size of your first shelter! Slimes can't actually hurt you, but when they get close enough, they'll push you around until you kill them all. Don't engage them near lava, cliffs or creepers. (Slimes drop 'slimeballs', which can be made cool 'sticky pistons'. Make sure and collect them whenever you can!) *Recent updates have made slimes able to spawn in swamps above ground, too.

Cave Spiders

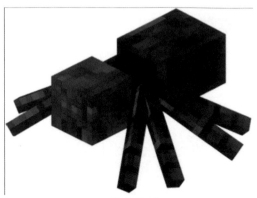

Cave Spiders

It's another spider! This one is smaller, meaner and much more aggressive than its above-ground cousin. Cave spiders only spawn in abandoned mineshafts, but even a pair of them can be very dangerous. You'll know a cave spider-nest is about when you find gobs of cobwebs covering the walls and ceilings. (Make sure you always have a sword handy to cut your way out of the webs!) Cave spiders are fast enough that using a bow isn't always recommended. When fighting one, keep an eye out for other monsters, as these mean arachnids are rarely found alone.

Now you know what lurks in the dark (but not in the Nether)... who cares! Let's mine!

Mining!

It's not just stone that you'll find underground, though you'll find plenty of that, but useful iron and gold ore, precious diamonds and even redstone (used for making circuitry and mechanical devices), and nigh-unbreakable obsidian, from which you can make a gateway to The Nether!

I'm not going to give away everything, but I've included some must-know facts below and some neat recipes to help you get started mining underground.

There's lots to see under, but lots of ways to get trapped, killed, lost or incinerated. Here are some basic tips:

- **Never dig straight down!**

Unless you know precisely what is under you (and most of the time you don't), avoid digging straight down unless you don't mind falling to your death. Sure, you'll be fine 95% of the time, but one long drop in lava and all your items are gone!

- **Never dig straight-up!**

This isn't nearly as dangerous as digging straight down, but digging straight up is a good way to drop sand blocks on your head (sand doesn't hold itself up), flood your mine or accidentally dig straight into some lava. If you see drips of red (lava) or (blue) coming from the blocks overhead, think twice before digging into them.

- **Always bring food!**

Starving to death is never fun. Starving to death lost and confused in your own mine is embarrassing and a great way to lose all the stuff in your inventory. Bring at least a couple food items down into the mine to snack on so you can regenerate your health if you get attacked.

- **Always bring light!**

Can you mine in the dark? Sure, if you want to be swarmed by monsters. Remember: monsters spawn in the darkness and it's easy to get lost.

- **Don't be stingy with the lights!**

If you make sure and dot your underground walls with a torch every 6 or 7 blocks, you should be able to make your supplies of torches last a while and keep your mine (largely) free of pesky creepers and zombies.

- **Always bring a weapon!**

You can fight without a sword or a bow, but you'll get hurt and need to eat more often. Don't find yourself fighting for your life far away from home!

- **Always bring wood!**

Almost everything you need can be found underground, with the exception of food and wood. Unless you're exploring an abandoned mineshaft, wood is very scarce underground and you can't make new tools, workbenches or torches without wood. Always carry a stack or so to avoid unnecessary trips to the surface.

- **Always bring a bucket of water!**

Why? Are you going to get thirsty? Nope, but if you step in a lava-pit, you'll be glad you did. Water turns lava into obsidian or cobblestone and can put you out if you catch on fire, Burning to death isn't fun and dying in lava is even worse: all your items (except your diamonds) will be destroyed instantly!

- **Dig Deeper!**

The best ores can only be found near bedrock that separates the Underground from the Nether (How do you get there? Make a gate from Obsidian and light it with a flint and steel. I'll let you figure out the particulars). Diamond and redstone are only found within 20-or-so block from the very bottom of the map!

- **Upgrade your tools!**

Some ores can only be extracted with certain pickaxes. Stone can be broken, but not collected by-hand. Iron ore can only be collected with a stone-or-better pickaxe and gold/diamond can only be collected with an iron-or-better pickaxe. Obsidian is even hard to mine...

- **A compass is a good idea!**

You can build yourself a compass with iron and redstone that will point you back to where you first entered the game. This is handy for point you back to familiar territory when you get turned around exploring underground.

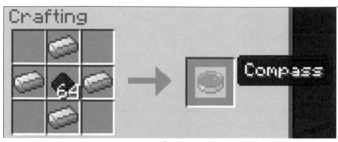

Compass

- **Mark your trails!**

It's easy to get lost underground, but if you mark your trails, you can easily find your way out. I always place torches on the left-hand side of the walls as I explore, so when I get turned around I just have to follow the torches to my right to know I'm headed back in the right (get in?) direction.

Heading In

Heading Out

- **Be (very) careful around lava!**

Glowing red lava can set you on fire with just a touch and, if you take a swim in it, will kill you in seconds! What's worse, if you die in or near lava, the items in your inventory can be destroyed.

Lava

So you're trapped.

Okay, so you're lost and turned around and you have no idea where 'back' is. You have a couple options:

1) Build a compass: If you have 4 iron ingots and 1 redstone and a crafting table, you can make yourself a compass to show you which way to dig back to spawn.

1. 2) Dig straight up and drop blocks underneath you as you jump.

This is generally a last-ditch escape effort. It's not recommended except when you're desperate. You're basically building a tower underneath you as fast as you're digging out the ceiling. Precarious and not always advised. The only thing worse than losing your items underground is losing them trapped somewhere within a solid block of stone. It's the fastest way to the surface, but you're also digging blind. (Are you sure there's not lava above right above you?)

Useful Mining Recipes

Minecraft is full of neat things for you to build. So many, in fact, that, unless you want to do a lot more reading, I couldn't list them here without boring you to death (which is an event that should be saved for the Creepers, naturally). Here are a couple neat things for you to play with, anyhow:

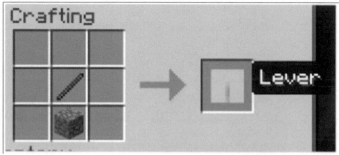

Lever: Try it with a Power Mine Rail!

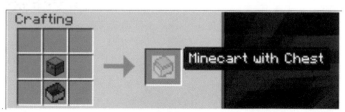

Mobil Storage

A Self-Propelled Minecart! Just add Coal!

Furnace: Turn your ores into ingots!

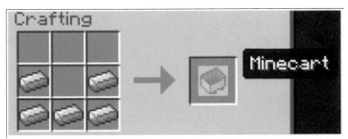

Minecart: Right Click to Ride the Rails!

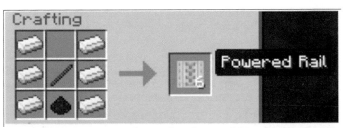

Powered Rail: In Minecraftia, rail pushes you! (Try attaching a redstone torch to it!)

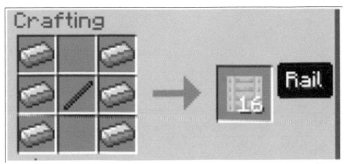

Rails: Just add a mine-cart for fast underground travel!

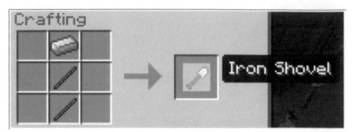

Iron Shovel: Dirt, can you dig it?

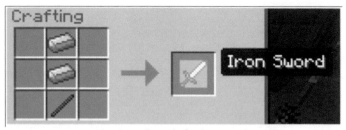

Iron Sword: Back, foul creeper! Back!

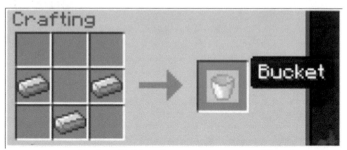

Bucket: Hold and transport water and lava!

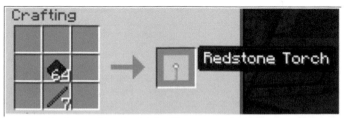

Redstone Torch: Think of it as a magical battery-wand.

Farming - Time to Eat!

Oh man! I bet you're hungry! Whenever you run, attack or jump your hunger gauge will drop faster than normal. (You'll eventually get hungry just standing around, but it takes much longer.) There are quite a few ways to keep yourself fed. Let's have a look:

Farming

Growing your own food can be fun! The first thing you'll need it a hoe:

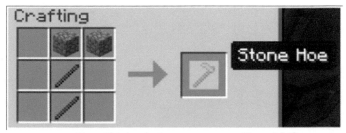

Hoe: This is what you were expecting, right?

Right click on a grassy-dirt block (these are only found in direct sunlight). You'll see the dirt turn into a plowed section of earth. Neat, eh? You'll plant seeds in these patches, but first you'll need some seeds. Head out into your nearest forest or plain and start knocking down tall grasses. You'll eventually get a handful of seeds. Head back to near your shelter and pick a nice sunny patch of ground. (Plants need light to grow. The more light the better.) Hoe the ground and plant your seeds!

All done? Almost. Plants grow fastest when they are near a source of water. Grab a bucket and head to the nearest water source and fill it up. Come back, dig a little trench near your tilled field and dump out the water. You should see your tilled patches turn a darker shade of brown as the water saturates the field!

Now you can wait! In about 5 minutes, under excellent conditions, you should have your first crop of wheat!

Wait, is the wheat ready? Plants grow in stages, from seed to completed crop. If you harvest too early, you won't get any wheat or seeds back. Let's look at the stages of growth:

Wheat Stages

Go ahead and wait until all your wheat is grown and then turn it into some bread!

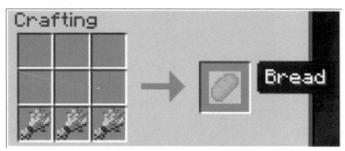

Bread: No baking involved!

Now you're a farmer! Well done!
But wait... there's more!

Want to do a little more farming? Don't get too excited, but you can also farm:
- **Potatoes**
  - ☐ Either steal some from your local village or look for your first potato as a rare drop from a zombie!
- **Carrots**

  ☐ Same as potatoes! (I have no idea why zombies eat so healthy.)
- **Sugar Cane**
  - ☐ Much easier to find, sugar cane grows next to water on either dirt, sand or grass blocks. Sugar cane can be used to make paper!
- **Pumpkins**
  - ☐ Look for these pre-carved jack'o'lanterns on any biome with grass. Wear them as a neat hat (Enderman aren't fans, for some reason), add a candle to spookily light-up-the-night or use them to build golems! (Maybe make a pie with eggs and sugar?)

Villages

Feeling a bit lonely? Don't be! You're not alone in Minecraftia! Though it might take a bit of looking, somewhere in the vast wilderness of are villages full of long-nosed friends just waiting to be made. (And traded with! You have found emeralds already, right? No? Check for hints towards the back of the guide. They're out there!)

If you're looking to find your first village without too much fuss, a couple of quick hints:

- **Villages are only found above ground.**
- **Villages only exist in the plains or in the desert.**
    - If you're seeing sky-scraping trees, fields of snow and ice or find yourself in a parallel dimension (which sometimes happens) you'll need to look elsewhere.

Village Ho!

Well, look what we have here! A little town full of huts, houses, shops, farms and even a well that the villagers can gather around and gossip about that strange man who keeps breaking into their homes and stealing their vegetables. (How rude!)

Let's say hello!

Villagers

Just another day in the village

These are the locals! (Don't stare!) Once known as 'Testificates', these villagers live, work and recreate all within the confines of their quaint little homesteads. They're happy to let you explore their villages in peace, as long as you don't hurt them. Villagers themselves won't stand and fight if you attack (they won't even stand outside in the rain!), but they're happy to let their golems put the hurt on you.

Iron Golem

Beware an angry iron golem! These peaceful man-shaped machines can normally be found wandering outside in medium-to-large sized villages. While golems are normally happy to stamp about aimlessly, their resistance to damage and high strength are put to good use in defending the village from aggressive players (but not you, right?) and the occasional zombie-siege. (Zombies love to try to eat villagers. Watch them try. It's great fun.) Stay on their good side or you'll wish you walked into a creeper.

Hint: I almost forgot! You can make your own golems! You'll need 1 pumpkin and 4   blocks of iron [hint: not ingots].

Trading

Tired of making everything yourself? Do the villagers have a deal for you!

If you walk up to a villager and right-click on him, a trading window will pop-up and you can see what items this particular villager has for trade and what he's willing to trade for.

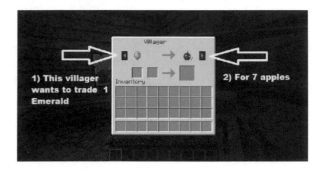

The trading window, pictured below, is similar to the crafting window. On the top-left, you'll see what a particular villager wants from you (1) and on the top-right is what he will give you in exchange (2).

The villager in the picture above wants one emerald from me and will trade 7 apples in exchange. Not the best deal, but each villager will offer you a different trade, so go right-clicking around town until you find something more to your liking.

Villager Professions

All villagers like to watch zombies get flattened by their pet golems, hate inclement weather, but not all of them are socialistic layabouts: some even have jobs! Good for them, right? Well, good for you, too, and here's why.

Villagers with jobs will trade you job-specific items!

But how can you tell what villager has what job? Good question, you'd think they might actually do some work that might give you a hint, but no, the just wander about with their arms stuck in their sweatshirts/apron/onesie-thing.

Villagers' professions can be distinguished by the color of their clothing.

Strange, I know, but here's a breakdown of professions and what items they offer:

Farmer Villager - *Brown Robe*

Buys: Wheat, Wool, Raw Chicken, Fish and Gold Ingots (rare).

Sells: Bread, Melon Slices, Apples, Cookies, Shears, Flint and Steel, Cooked Chicken, Arrows and Flint.

Librarian Villager - *White Robe*

Buys: Paper, Books, Written Books, Gold Ingots (rare)

Sells: Bookshelves, Glass, Compasses, Clocks.

Priest Villager - *Pink/Fuchsia Robe

Buys: Gold Ingots.

Sells: Eye of Ender, Bottle o' Enchanting, Redstone, Glowstone
*Enchants: Weapons and Armor (both uncommon).

Blacksmith Villager - *Brown Underclothing with Black Apron*

Buys: Coal/Charcoal, Iron Ingots, Gold Ingots, Diamonds.

Sells: Iron Weapons and Armor, Diamond Weapons and Armor, Chainmail Weapons and Armor (rare).

Butcher Villager - *Brown Underclothing with White Apron*

Buys: Coal/Charcoal, Raw Porkchops, Raw Beef, Gold Ingot (rare).

Sells: Saddles, Leather Armor, Cooked Porkchop, Steak.

Furry Friends

If you'd like some companionship, but can't seem to convince the villagers to follow you out on your grand adventure, don't fret. While most things out in the wilds of Minecraftia are out to get you (or at least wish you'd leave them alone), there are two types of wild animals you can:

wolves and **ocelots.**

The Majestic Wolf

While having a wolf follow you around sounds like a good idea, it's really not: mostly because they won't. Wolves can be found in forests or taiga biomes on any difficulty and will happily eat any sheep that can't escape their 4-legged clutches. (Are there a lot of mysterious wool blocks popping up in your sheep pen? You might be keeping a local wolf well-fed.)

So what does a lonely miner/adventurer/master builder like yourself do to get a wolf to lay off those sheep and love you? One word: bones. Wolves love the things. Save up a couple bones (at least 3) and go searching for your soon-to-be furry companion. Once you find a wolf, go up to him and right-click him while hold a bone. It might take a few bones, but, once you see a red collar appear around his neck, you'll soon have your very own dog!

Your new best friend will follow you everywhere you go (sometimes to an aggravating degree) and can be told to sit (right-click) or follow (right-click, again, while he's sitting). Sometimes keeping your pooch sitting near your bed or at the entrance to your mine is a better idea than letting him roam. Pets can be killed by monsters, lava and other perils, so think twice about where you're headed before

The Also Majestic Ocelot

The ocelot is the wild cousin of the cat and, like the wolf, until this nimble little guy is tamed, he won't have anything to do with you. Ocelots are harder to find than wolves and generally only spawn in jungles, often high in the trees. Ocelots are fond of killing and eating chickens, which they will slowly stalk from behind, but actively avoid almost everything else in the game, including you.

To tame an ocelot you'll need a few raw fish and some patience. Ocelots are skittish and cannot be tamed while they are actively trying to escape you. To successfuly tame one, you need to hold a raw fish and wait for the wild cat to approach you. One its within range, right-click the ocelot to tame it. (Make sure you're not hungry, you'll eat the fish yourself and scare off the cat.)

Once tame, your new kitty will lose its spotted coat and follow you around, mewling happily. Unlike dogs, cats tend to roam around the area they're told to stay in and enjoy getting in your way by sitting on beds and construction benches.

It's usually a good idea to keep a cat near your favourite entrance to your home. Creepers have a natural (and inexplicable) fear of cats and will do whatever they can to escape them.

Hunting

So you're more of a hunter than a gatherer, eh?

Well, hunting is pretty straight-forward: find a pig, cow, or chicken and kill it. Then cook the meat that drops in a Furnace. Repeat as necessary and eat until you're stuffed.

Cooked meat is much more filling than raw is, but you're welcome to eat either. (Though you might get a stomach-ache from the raw stuff.)

(Oh: you can also breed your own animals for slaughter. Try farming up some wheat and offering to animals. You might also be able to pen them in with fencing, which I'm sure couldn't be made with the right configuration of Sticks...)

Enchanting & Brewing

Enchanting

Enchanting Bench: Could those Bookshelves be for more than decoration... ?

Did you know you can make your tools, weapons and armor even better? Remember that experience bar we talked about earlier? (The green segmented-line at the bottom of the screen?) Well, here is where you cash in all that experience for enchantments that make your tools last long and drop more goodies from ore blocks, your weapons sharper and stronger, and your armor protect your from fire and poison.

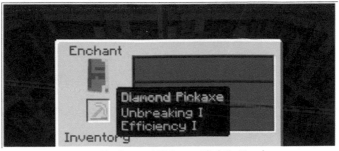

Enchanted Pickaxe: Slightly Used

Once you know how to mine Obsidian, to make bookshelves and have collected some redstone, you'll have everything you need to make an enchanting bench. Again, this guide is more for new players and I don't want to ruin the fun by telling you how to do everything, but you'll find some hints about collecting Obsidian and redstone in the Mining section, and I'll just say now that bookcases are made with wood, and books are made of paper, which is made of sugar. I'll let you figure out the rest. Get to your workbench and start experimenting!

What enchantments are available, you ask?

Well, since you asked nicely:

Armor Enchantments
- **Protection** – reduces damage from most sources.
- **Fire Protection** – asbestos underwear, more or less.
- **Feather Falling** – reduced damage from falls.
- **Blast Protection** – bane of creepers everywhere.
- **Projective Protection** – arrows, fireballs and the like sting a little less.
- **Respiration** – makes able to hold your breath a little longer.
- **Aqua Affinity** – mine faster underwater.
- **Thorns** – your armor hurts whatever is hurting you.
- **Unbreaking** – lowers the chance that your armor is damaged when used.

Sword Enchantments
- **Sharpness** – extra damage.
- **Smite** – extra damage to the undead.
- **Bane of Arthropods** – extra damage to spiders and insect(-ish) creatures
- **Knockback** – knocks back enemies when you hit them.
- **Fire Aspect** – light bad things on fire.

- **Looting** – baddies may drop more loot/increases rare item drops.
- **Unbreaking** – lowers the chance that your armor is damaged when used.

Tool Enchantments

- **Efficiency** – gathers resources more quickly.
- **Silk Touch** – (My personal favorite) blocks mined will drop themselves, even when something else should drop. (Try mining stone. No more cobblestone for you!)
- **Unbreaking** – lowers the chance that your armor is damaged when used.
- **Fortune** – change to multiply items dropped/mined/gathered.

Bow Enchantments

- **Unbreaking** – lowers the chance that your armor is damaged when used.
- **Power** – extra damage.
- **Punch** – same as knockback.
- **Flame** – sets your arrows, and sometime bad guys, on fire.
- **Infinity** – infinite arrows as long as you have 1 arrow in your inventory.

Enchanting Hints: Remember, higher-quality enchantments require more XP than lower-quality enchantment. (More bookshelves, too.) You don't have to risk your life to get XP from killing monsters, though that is arguably the fastest way to go about it without resorting to a 'mob grinder'. Mining certain blocks will also reward you with XP, so don't feel like you have to brave the dark night just for best enchantments.

Brewing

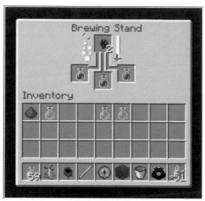

Brewing Stand

Want to make poisons, do you? Well you better get yourself a cauldron (which I'm SURE isn't made out of iron), a brewing stand (which CAN'T be made out of stone and a hard-to find item, called a *cough* blaze rod *cough*, from the Nether), and some bottles (which, incidentally are made from melted glass...).

Well, I don't want to give too much away, but you can find ingredients for you potions all over Minecraftia. From monsters drops, to redstone, to food items and more.

Be Your Own Blacksmith! The Anvil

Want to rename your favorite sword something clever? ('The Stabber', maybe?), or just repair your enchanted diamond pickaxe? Well, industrious player, you're going to need an anvil! As you can imagine, making an anvil requires a lot of metal.

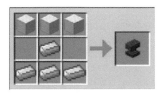

Here's your do-it-yourself anvil construction list:

1. **31 ingots of iron**
2. **Craft an iron block out of 9 ingots of iron. (Protip: If the crafting bench is full of iron, you're probably doing it right.)**
3. **Make 2 more blocks of iron.**
4. **Assemble the 3 iron blocks and remaining 4 iron ingots like so:**
5. **Anvil!**

Well done! Let's get to smithing! Right click on all that metal!

Anvil Crafting Window

Okay, so now that you've wasted all that iron, what are you to do? Well, you might try:

1. **Rename your items!**
   1. Plop the weapons to be renamed in the leftmost square (just under the pixelated hammer).
   2. Click on the 'Name' box (just below the 'Repair & Name' text)
   3. Type something!
2. **Repair your items!**
   1. **Either**
      1. Put the item to be repaired in the leftmost square and one of its core components in the middle square (iron ingots for iron items, diamonds for diamond tools, etc.) **or,**
      2. Put an identical item in the middle square (an iron sword MUST have an iron sword; a diamond axe MUST have a diamond axe, etc.)
         1. Hint: Renamed items will not repair as much as an item with its original name.
   2. And then left-click on the item in the rightmost box to complete the repair!
3. **Combine 2 Magical Items into 1 Really Enchanted Item!**
   1. The enchanted item in the leftmost box is the 'target item', which means this is where the enchantments are going to end up.
   2. The item you put in the middle box is going to be destroyed and its enchantments will end up on the enchanted item in the leftmost box.
      1. Be sure you don't mix the two up.

Is that all? Do I know all there is to know about anviling, now?

Well, not really. To tell you the truth, its sort of complicated and you'll probably learn more by messing about than anything else, so I won't ruin the semi-educational process for you, but I will give you a couple more things to think about when you're anvil'ing away:

- **You can damage your anvil.**
    - In fact, you probably will. It's okay. It's a fact of life. No one is blaming you, but every time you use your anvil there is a small chance you're going to bang it up some.
- **Anvils can't fly.**
    - Neither can sand. Maybe they're cousins?
- **Magical items are easier to repair with other magical items.**
    - Repairing 'The Stabber' with all its magical enchantments is going to take more than basic items to really put a polish on its blade.
- **Repairing costs XP.**
    - I did mention that, I hope. Because it does.

Repairing/combining damaged items makes the repair/enchantment less effective (well, not the enchantment, but the durability of the finished enchanted item... try it out, you'll see what I

Redstone Circuits

or "What The Heck Am I Doing?" for Advanced Users

Redstone Circuit with Repeaters

So you found all that redstone underground and don't know what to do with it. It can't be made into tools, weapons, armor or food, so what the heck is it for?

Try spreading some redstone dust on the ground. See how it spreads out in lines? Redstone dust is the Minecraftia equivalent of wire! Redstone torches (made just like regular torches, except with redstone), along with buttons (made from cobblestone), levels and pressure plates will send a pulse of power to attached resdtone circuits.

But what can you power? Well:
- Doors,
- Powered Rails (see above),
- Pistons,
- Trap doors,
- Dispensers,
- Fence Gates,
- Noteblocks.

Here are some of the more complex recipes to help you get started with your redstone experiments:

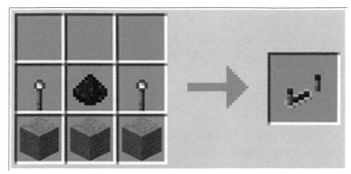

Repeater

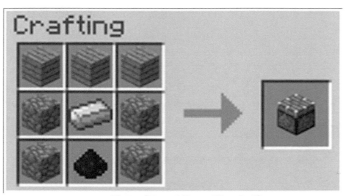

Piston (Try adding a Slimeball)

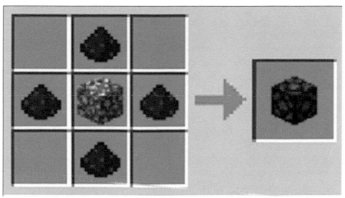

Redstone Lamp (Redstone Lamp + Glowstone Block)

Mine Craft

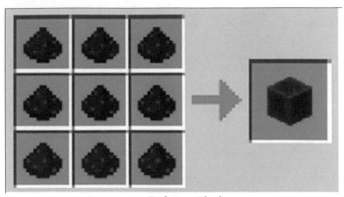

Redstone Block

So... now what?

Minecraft technically has an ending, but most players aren't in any hurry to 'beat' the game. And you shouldn't be, either. Even if you mastered everything in this guide (well done, if so!) you've got plenty more to explore.

Here are a few ideas to keep you busy..

Thar's Emerald in them thar Extreme Hills!

Emeralds - Minecraftian Currency

You've probably noticed that villagers like to trade for emerald. Who can blame them? Emerald is one of the rarest ores in the game and can only be naturally mined in the 'Extreme Hills' biome. You never need to mine any emerald yourself, as villagers are happy to trade them for your goods, but if you want to dig this precious ore out of the ground yourself, you'll need to start looking for a hilly landscape full of massive cliffs, deep valleys and blueish-grey grass. Dig down deep enough to find gold and, sooner or later, you'll find the rare emerald ore blocks.

Behold! There be green ore in these hills!

Behold, again! Emerald riches!

Wood you like to decorate?

From left-to-right: Oak, Spruce, Birch and Jungle wood.

When decorating, remember that different types of trees drop different colored types of wood, which can be turned into planks, stairs and more. Don't get stumped with just one type of wood!

Keep a journal!

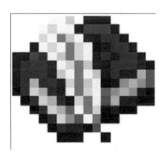

Dear Minecraft Diary,

Want to keep a written log of your various adventures? A shopping list the next time your need to stop by the village to trade? Close that .doc file and throw a Book into your crafting bench with an ink sac and a feather and become a published Minecraft author! It's just that easy.

Remember: When you're penning your epic tale, 'Done' saves what you've written ...while 'Sign' finalizes the book. Once you Sign the book, you can't write anymore.

Temples

What's this? An abandoned temple? I bet nothing interesting is in there

Spot a curious mossy-covered structure deep in the wilds of the jungle? Spy a half-buried pyramid in the desert wastes? Treasure (and possibly traps) await adventurous explorers who venture within these forgotten temples. Loot found within is random, but chests will occasionally contain rare and valuable emeralds used for trading with the locals.

The Mysterious Ender Chest

With that much purple magic, you know it's gotta be cool.

The magical teleportation powers of the mysterious Endermen can now be harnessed by the craftiest of craftsmen. The ender chest allows all items placed within it to be available from any other ender chest, no matter the distance or dimension.

Want to keep your favorite set of armor available in your distant base, but don't want to carry it all the way there? No problem! Just build an ender chest at end location and never worry about packing materials in between again!

Crafting Hint: Ender chests require a good deal of obsidian and one *Eye of Ender* each,   so make sure you stock up!

Tripwires and Tripwire Hooks

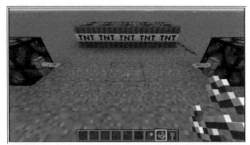

I bet nothing bad would happen if you walked into that...

Want to rig a dastardly trap to keep monsters out of your home? Break out the string and let's set up a tripwire! Like redstone, sting can be run along the ground by holding it in your hand and right-clicking on the ground. Unlike redstone, string can be used to connect two blocks separated by some distance. Think of a clothesline to get a good mental image. Since you can't dry your clothes in Minecraft, we'll have to find something else to do with all this string... like attach it to a tripwire hook

Tripwire hooks are basically anchors that connect your tripwire ('clothesline') to other blocks. You can connect a tripwire to a lever, a redstone pulse generator (see the section on redstone for more) or to a few blocks of TNT, if you like your traps to be a bit-more straightforward.

Yet-another Crafting Hint: You'll need one iron ingot, one stick and one wooden plank to get your tripwire trap off the ground. ('Off the ground'... get it? Nevermind.)

Reuse! Recycle... in the furnace!

Do you have some old wooden tools from ages back that are cluttering up your storage area? Toss them in the furnace the next time you're smelting!

Don't Break It! Silk Touch it, instead!

Certain blocks can only be collected with the help of this handiest-of-enchantments - Silk Touch.

You normally can't collect *grass*, *ore blocks*, *ice* or remove items like the *Ender Chest* after they been placed without breaking them into different parts. The Silk Touch enchantment changes all that! Try it out!

Remember: You still have to use the correct tool for the job, ie: an 'Silk Touch' enchanted axe won't be able to collect ore blocks (or even ore).

Beware the Nether Portal!

Monsters lurking just beyond the portal to the Nether may pop on through to see how you are doing, compliment you on your lovely home and maybe kill you while they're at it. Don't feel too safe on this side of the portal!

Remember: If you're playing on the safer difficulties, zombie pigmen and the like won't sneak through the portals to attack, but they will probably judge you from the depths.

Updates

Updates come along to add new features to the game every couple weeks and playing online is a different type of experience altogether. (In fact, parts of this guide might be outdated , though most information should be accurate.)

Play with Friends Online! - Start up a multiplayer server with some friends, or join one of hundreds of active servers online. There are tons of user-made mods that add new rules and items to turn 'vanilla' Minecraft into a whole new experience. There are zombie-survival servers, RPG servers, Creative servers (where you can build to your heart's content), Hardcore (1-death and that's it) servers, PvP servers and much, much more. Check out the forums on Minecraft.net for more info.

Creative Mode - Want to just build, build, build? Try Creative Mode from the Main Menu. You don't have to worry about dying or monsters and can instantly spawn any type of block, or, animal or monster you want. Build whole cities, ocean liners, skyscrapers, or anything else you can imagine.

Here are a few ideas:

Make your own abandoned crypt:

Or maybe a jungle outpost.

Or how about just a giant creeper statue made of gold?:

Updates come along to add new features to the game every couple weeks and playing online is a different type of experience altogether. (In fact, parts of this guide might be outdated already, though most information should be accurate.)

Start up a multiplayer server with some friends, or join one of hundreds of active servers online. There are tons of user-made mods that add new rules and items to turn 'vanilla' Minecraft into a whole new experience. There are zombie-survival servers, RPG servers, Creative servers (where you can build to your heart's content), Hardcore (1-death and that's it) servers, PvP servers and much, much more. Check out the forums on Minecraft.net for more info.

Want to just build, build, build? Try Creative Mode from the Main Menu. You don't have to worry about dying or monsters and can instantly spawn any type of block, or, animal or monster you want. Build whole cities, ocean liners, skyscrapers, or anything else you can imagine.

Hardcore Mode - Want to try something harder? Hardcore Mode is just like normal Survival (the mode described in this guide), but you only get one life. Just one long fall, one too-many arrows to the head or an unlucky dip in lava and the game is over: upon death your hardcore world is erased. Sounds serious, right? It's intense. Give it a try if you feel like you've mastered Minecraftia.

Keep Up-to-Date! - The Mojang team is fairly active on Twitter and occasional stops by the Minecraft sub-Reddit on reddit.com: www.reddit.com/r/minecraft. Get the low-down on new mods, epic buildings and servers that other Minecrafters are working on here.

###

About The Author

David Oconner has been writing and publishing books on many of his varied interests. He has books on topics such as Cichlid Fish, How to Grow Tomatoes, Sugar Gliders, How to Play Minecraft and more.

18189217R00034

Made in the USA
Charleston, SC
21 March 2013